Graham Lacey has been giver
appreciates and comprehend
vide real, practical, powerful
help to people through the gi
be useful to the Master through this priceless supernatural gift.

—Rolland & Heidi Baker
Iris Global, Mozambique

Jesus chose twelve men who were nobodies to change the world. In fact, they turned the world upside down. Without the helps ministry the church has no future. Not one of the twelve disciples were in full time ministry. Jesus used fishermen, tax collectors and tent makers to reinforce His ministry on earth. (Jesus Himself was a country carpenter by trade). This is the time when the helper is going to be used to usher in the Kingdom of God, like never before. This is the book that captures the ministry of the helper unlike any other before.

—Angus Buchan
Farmer, Evangelist, Author, South Africa

THE GIFT OF HELPS stirred me deeply. I loved Dr. Lacey's rich employment of personal stories, hymns, poetry, quotations, and scriptural promises. But above that, he ignites spiritual understanding on this rarely mentioned gift, and woos the reader to respond with Spirit-empowered help. This book is a call to the ministry of helps - to those drawn by the brooding of the Spirit to encourage, love, pray and share all one possesses for the benefit of others.

—Jeff Farmer
President, Pentecostal/Charismatic Churches of North America

Graham Lacey has helped each of us to go up in our leadership through his new outstanding book, THE GIFT OF HELPS. When this book is released, I will do all I can to share copies of it with other leaders. These pages are filled and overflowing with leadership gold.

—Dr. Ronnie Floyd
CEO, Executive Committee of the
Southern Baptist Convention (2019-2021)
Pastor Emeritus, Cross Church, Arkansas

In his book, THE GIFT OF HELPS, Dr. Lacey gives both biblical and practical ways to overcome the narcissism that is so prevalent today and to begin the journey toward spiritual health, experiencing God's assistance and blessings. Remember that the Lord will reward each one of us for the good we do (EPHESIANS 6:8 NLT). As you begin to incorporate the principles in this book into your life, prepare to be blessed as you bless others.

—Alton Garrison
Assistant General Superintendent (2007-2019),
The General Council of the Assemblies of God

If you've been seeking to know your God-given assignment in life, read THE GIFT OF HELPS. Drawing on the richness of his own experience with God and some of the most powerful scriptures in the bible, Graham sheds a flood of practical insight on the much needed and often overlooked subject. Discover your spiritual identity and begin to operate in your God-given gift.

—Bob Gass (1944-2019)
Author of *The Word For Today*

The spiritual gift of helps is a vital ministry of support for the Body of Christ. That is why I'm very glad that my good friend Dr. Graham Lacey has written a book that addresses the need for the discovery and deployment of this wonderful gift. God's gifts keep on giving through his people and strengthen His church as we exercise our faith. The helping gifts are a blessing to so many and I commend Dr. Lacey's book to you as you devote your life serving Christ and His church.

—Dr. Jack Graham
Pastor, Prestonwood Baptist Church, Plano, Texas

In a day when many believers seldom seek to discover much less use their own spiritual gifts, my lifelong friend, Graham Lacey has raised the awareness of their importance in his new book THE GIFT OF HELPS. Somewhere there is something for you to do, as no one can do quite like you can, because you are uniquely gifted by God. Consume these pages and begin the great adventure of partnership with God. Read it and reap!

—Dr. OS Hawkins
President/CEO, GuideStone Financial Resources, Dallas, Texas

Dr. Graham Lacey seems to be tailor made to pen this book on a much-neglected subject, THE GIFT OF HELPS. He has spent a lifetime supporting, encouraging, and serving some of our great spiritual heroes; from Dr. Billy Graham, Doug Coe, Bill Bright, and even to our beloved patriarch Dr. W. A. Criswell. This book is practical, biblical and inspiring. We don't have to be a legend to do acts worthy of being a hero.

—Dr. Robert Jeffress
Sr. Pastor, First Baptist Church, Dallas, Texas

Graham Lacey's book on the gift of helps will encourage every Christian. He shows how the least of the gifts are needed as much as the high-profile gifts. It is written by a layman who knows his Bible backward and forward—probably better than many ordained ministers. Those who only know Graham as an international business man may be surprised at the depth and breadth of his knowledge. But with his Brethren background plus being tutored by his uncle Prof. David Gooding (one of the great Bible scholars of our time), he has produced a book that should be read around the world.

—Dr. R.T. Kendall
Minister, Westminster Chapel (1977-2002)

While many of the more charismatic gifts have been frequently elevated and taught on, the gifts of helps have often been woefully neglected. In his new book, THE GIFT OF HELPS, Dr. Graham Lacey masterfully illuminates the beauty and necessity of this often-undervalued gift, without which effective ministry is impossible. Whether you are a senior leader or serving in a supportive role, THE GIFT OF HELPS is a vital resource for your ministry.

—Evangelist Daniel Kolenda
President and CEO, Christ for all Nations

Graham Lacey shares his God given epiphanies in this marvelous book, THE GIFT OF HELPS. In it we grasp more clearly the Character of God our Father, who Himself is the source and administrator of this prescient, discerning gift. Since the fall of man, God's ready response to human need has always been, help. Those who call upon his name and turn to Him when all helpers flee, have always found in him, unfailing help. In this heartfelt transparent book, he shares how God delights in sharing His fondness for helping, by using us as conduits of His splendid help. After reading it I came away with the deepened conviction; if we are led by His Spirit, God will use us to reach down into the hollows of human misery and help those who cannot help themselves; while always bearing witness, it is ever; "His help." I pray you will find this book itself, a gift of helps, helping all who read its pages know more of the tender, gracious, giving Character of God.

—Wintley Phipps
Founder & President, U.S. Dream Academy

It has been my privilege to know Dr. Graham Lacey, and his family for 40 years. I knew immediately that this highly successful businessman would be someone who could teach me more than I could ever imagine about leadership. He has experiences unlike anyone I have ever met, with connections in the highest levels of business and political acumen. This man has taught me the real secret of being a leader, and that is to be a servant leader. I have watched his generosity of time, energy, and finances used to encourage, uplift, and save lives around the world. I know of no-one who is more highly qualified to write a book on THE GIFT OF HELPS than my brother Graham. As you read this wonderful book, fasten your seatbelt because it will take you places you never dreamed of going.

—Dr. Jay Strack
President & Founder, Student Leadership University,
Orlando, Florida

GRAHAM LACEY

The GIFT of HELPS

MAYFLOWER
— PUBLISHING —

MAYFLOWER
— PUBLISHING —

Published by Mayflower Publishing Ltd
www.mayflowerpublishing.com

ISBN: 978-1-913771-00-3 (paperback)
ISBN: 978-1-913771-01-0 (epub)

Cover design by Erik Peterson and Jonathan Wentworth
Editor: David Teems

DEDICATION

In April 2010, I commenced the first of a number of hospital stays, culminating in a final stay of six weeks. One year later, still suffering severe clinically-resistant chronic depression, away from my family and the subsequent collapse of all my businesses, I continued my slow recovery in London as the guest of both Paul Szkiler and Michael Fitch, awesome brothers in the Lord, and so patient and so very generous.

During this time, I received a telephone call from a good friend of mine, Richard Akitt, from the Isle of Man. He requested that I meet him for dinner that evening at a restaurant in London. Unwell, I declined, but undeterred, Richard refused to accept my decision, informing me that he had something very important to share, and so we met. During the meal, he said many things, but the significant message was this, "I am here for you, for Susan, and your sons Luke and James."

I know what it means to go the second mile, and Richard has gone the seventh. He is a walking, talking, sharing, praying, caring, giving manifestation of the Biblical 1 Corinthians 12:28 gift of helps. He is not seen even though he is six foot eight. Although he wears gloves of love made with the leather of humility, his fingerprints are everywhere. His wife Marlene, and daughters JoJo and Danielle not surprisingly are as beautiful inside as they are outside.

It is therefore my honor to dedicate this book to Richard Akitt, for all he has done for my family and me, by exercising the gift of helps.

I am also grateful for the *helps* of our brothers and sisters in Christ from the United Kingdom, United States, South Africa, Northern Ireland, Australia, Isle of Man, and beyond who came and surrounded my wife Susan and our sons while I was hospitalized and away from home for so long.

—Graham Lacey

ACKNOWLEDGMENTS

I would like to acknowledge the invaluable contribution of Barry Sneed, who has been with me on the journey of The Gift of Helps from its inception.

And with great thankfulness, I want to acknowledge Jonathan Wentworth for understudying, scribing, praying, encouraging, loving, sharing his input, and so effectively living out his gift of helps.

—Graham Lacey

CONTENTS

PREFACE

I am delighted my husband Graham asked me to write the preface for this book, THE GIFT OF HELPS. I have to admit I had never heard of this particular spiritual gift before, but on reading 1 CORINTHIANS 12:28, I have come to appreciate how important this gift of the Spirit is. As Graham says in his first chapter, helps is a patient, loving, and humble gift.

God had "His way" with Graham after he prayed every day for two years, "Take my life and let it be consecrated Lord to thee." As God lovingly broke my husband by removing his health and his entire wealth, He awesomely remolded him by His grace and love to become all he is today.

During this time, we both came into a completely different relationship with God. Our Heavenly Father drew us to Him through the power of His Holy Spirit, where we came to know Him rather than know about Him. What a loving Father we have! I am now so in love with God the Father, Jesus and the Holy Spirit.

The "helps" God sent us over many years were extraordinary men and women of God who walked alongside us in so many ways, each person with their own unique gift of encouraging, loving, praying and sharing. We will always be thankful to God and in awe and wonder of how He looked after us as a family during those many years of trial and tribulation, by sending His "helps" as God transformed my husband from a "Jacob" to an "Israel."

Thank you, Father, for your gift of HELPS.

—Susan Lacey

INTRODUCTION

On my spiritual journey, there are people whose contribution to my life can only be adequately rewarded, as will be the case, in heaven. As my writings declare, my late brother Adrian, who led me to Christ, set me on the path that has led me to write, enhanced by the life-long contribution of my beloved uncle, Prof. David Gooding, and the delightful introduction into my life during my time of illness and brokenness of Bob Gass and his wife, Debbie, founders of The Word For Today.

Bob and I enjoyed sharing with each other fresh thoughts from Scripture that "will preach," that is, what we believed would work well in a sermon. And it was a message he brought in Manchester, England, to the UK supporters of his outstanding ministry, about the (unnamed) men that held the ropes, lowering the basket for the Apostle Paul to escape almost certain death and continue his awesome ministry, that awoke in me a new realisation.

This emphasis on unnamed "helpers" who played a vital yet easily overlooked role led to me seeing the significance of the gift of helps in

1 Corinthians 12:28, and the dramatic example of a specific use of *helps* set out in Acts 27:17. This combination is what started me on my journey of discovering the essence of this vital gift.

This book, with its five principal chapters—*Helps, Encouraging, Loving, Praying, Sharing*—encapsulates all that God has shown me about the gift of helps, and I pray it both illuminates your understanding and inspires you to activate those gifts.

Chapter 1
HELPS

> Every good thing given and every perfect gift is from above, coming down from the Father of lights, with whom there is no variation or shifting shadow.
>
> —James 1:17 NASB

> Kindle afresh the gift of God which is in you.
>
> —2 Timothy 1:6 NASB

The English word, *helps*, is most often used and recognized as a verb, a word that suggests action. It makes something happen. It *does* something. In the context of Christian care, it does something quite wonderful, something divine. But not satisfied with mere action, this inspired little word also doubles as a noun. *Helps* is distinguished by the Apostle Paul as one of the gifts of the Holy Spirit.

> And God hath set some in the church, first apostles, secondarily prophets, thirdly teachers, after that miracles, then gifts of healings, helps, governments, diversities of tongues.
>
> —1 CORINTHIANS 12:28 KJV

In listing the spiritual gifts, Paul is not arbitrary, but specific. Some gifts are, indeed, greater than other gifts. The apostle ranks above the prophet, the prophet above the teacher, and so on. However, because of the unique economy of God, his *first-shall-be-last* economy, we are careful how we judge and consider these gifts. Dr. R. T. Kendall says *helps* "is the lowest profile gift, the most taken for granted (like the pancreas in the body) but essential for the body of Christ to function properly."[1]

Knowing and understanding his audience as the author of 1 CORINTHIANS did, including generations yet to come, while encouraging you and I to desire the higher gifts, and to desire them "earnestly," the distribution of these gifts is de-

---

1 R. T. KENDALL, MORE OF GOD: SEEK THE BENEFACTOR, NOT JUST THE BENEFITS, CHARISMA HOUSE, 2019.

termined not by our own choice or volition, but at the absolute discretion of the Holy Spirit. Divinely discerned, though utterly unmerited, *"Are all apostles?"* Paul asks, *"Are all prophets? Are all teachers? Do all work miracles? Do all possess gifts of healing? Do all speak with tongues? Do all interpret?"*[2]

The gifts of the Spirit are given for the edification and unity of the body of Christ. Therefore, dispersal of the gifts is determined by the Holy Spirit who gives them, who knows us better than we know ourselves, who knows how we work, how we think, how our instincts are driven. The gifts should not be perceived as an "a la carte" menu. Rather, it is for the Holy Spirit to determine, not for us to presume upon a particular gift. For the sake of clarity, these gifts may be divided into four categories.

TEACHING: apostles, prophets, and teachers
WONDER WORKING: miracles and healings
SERVING: *helps* and governments
SPEAKING: tongues and prophecy

These gifts are complementary, that is, they find their optimal expression in Christian community where each gift is cultivated and put to its highest and best use among the brethren.

---

2 1 CORINTHIANS 12:29-30

But that is not all.

I will say more about it later, but the gifts of the Spirit are empowered by love, which provides context for their use. The exercise of love brings about equilibrium in the application of the gifts, the divine balance. Indeed, love is the connective tissue, the paste that holds it all together, that gives them not only speech and action, but backbone.

Paul devotes an entire chapter (1 Corinthians 12) to illuminating the gifts of the spirit, why they are important, why we need them, how they function, how they are exercised, who allocates them, and so forth, then leads us to a summit, and shows us "*the most excellent way.*" *Helps* should be a manifestation of this love we are called to demonstrate. The passage below shows its characteristics, what *helps* is made of, and how it should be known and recognized in this world.

> Love is patient, love is kind. It does not envy, it does not boast, it is not proud. It is not rude, it is not self-seeking, it is not easily angered, it keeps no record of wrongs. Love does not delight in evil but rejoices with the truth. It always protects, always trusts, always hopes, always perseveres. Love never fails.
>
> —1 Corinthians 13:4-8a NIV

There are some gifts that, in light of the greater gifts, have been largely ignored. When did you last hear a sermon on the gift of helps?

WHAT IS HELPS?

Helps ministry, as Paul understood it, is a gift of service to others. It means to bring relief, to support, sympathize, serve, share, aid and assist others, by giving of ourselves to the body of Christ, and as a living testimony to the world. It is a willingness to do the most menial task with a spirit of humility and grace. And though an action may be seen only by the beneficiary, it is nonetheless celebrated and recorded in heaven.

Those involved in the ministry of *helps* are always ready to volunteer, to work around the church doing the mundane and least appealing jobs, and doing them faithfully and with great love. It may be a strategic or administrative support of one kind or another. It can be as an aid to the widowed, the elderly and infirm, or those in mourning. *Helps* comes alongside the downtrodden, downcast, depressed, defeated, doubting, and deserted and often meets humanity at its most primitive level.

> Those with the spiritual gift of helps have been given the unique ability to identify those who are struggling with doubt, fears, and other spiritual battles. They move toward those in spiritual need with a kind word, an understanding and compassionate demeanor, and the unique ability to speak scriptural truth in a convicting and loving fashion.
>
> —Dr. Charles Stanley

A study of the Bible reveals that collectively the words *help, helps, helper,* and *helpers* are used over 240 times. The Greek αντιλεψις [*antilepsis*], means "practical help, aid, lending support," that is, helping and doing so joyfully unto the Lord.

Helps are led by the Holy Spirit through the local representatives of Jesus, who, like Him, are full of love, prepared and joyful to serve, patient listeners with understanding hearts, who, through praying and sharing, impart encouragement from the scriptures. There are burdens that cannot and should not be carried alone, which is why *helps* is such a vital gift for us to pray for and exercise.

As it is with any gift of the Holy Spirit, it is an obligation for believers to activate this gift, with the understanding that it is not an option, but a command. Therefore, we need to prayerfully seek the Holy Spirit's leading as to who needs the gift of helps, for we are giving on His behalf and in

His strength, not our own. A pastor from London, when asked for his perspective on *helps,* said the following:

> The Spirit-given ability to help or assist others so that their needs are met or they can fulfil a particular task or ministry. The ability to discern and perform tasks or duties that release people to do ministry or pursue their calling. I have often said that if I had a dozen people with a genuine gift of helps then I could change the world. People with the gift of helps supernaturally discern what a leader or group needs to fulfil their ministry with excellence. They selflessly come alongside leaders, refusing any attention or praise, to help those leaders achieve great things or to maximize the leader's effectiveness. Often, people with a gift of helps may feel called to positions such as personal assistants and the like. I would boldly state that if you see any leader or ministry that has a significant impact beyond just their local context then they likely have one or more persons with the gift of helps working with them. The gift of helps is more than just the person who likes to help out and serve – something we're all called to do.
>
> —Rodney Woods, City Temple (London)

Though we often admire those in the spotlight, they too have need of support, however elevated and whatever their gift. For example, the game of basketball would be less thrilling without the occasional "assist," that is, for one player to pass the ball to another who is in a better position to score. This metaphor works well, for if the basket is made, both players enjoy the satisfaction of a score and the team benefits as well, each successful assist raising the hopes of a win.

We in the body of Christ, fulfilling the gift of helps, provide this necessary assistance. We are the "assists" in demonstrating the love of God. In so doing, we enable the scoring of basketball three-pointers (figuratively speaking) in our obedience to the Father, the Son, and the Holy Spirit. However, it is only in full reliance upon the help of God, by His Spirit, that this gift becomes effective.

The often-quoted phrase "*God helps those who help themselves*" is used readily by Christians and non-Christians alike, but it is not biblical. In fact, I believe it contradicts the Word of God. Benjamin Franklin, one of the founding fathers of the United States of America, popularized the misleading little proverb in his Poor Richard's Almanack (1757). As a deist, he did not believe in a personal God. A survey in America found that one in eight people thought this quote was from the ten commandments. The truth may be closer to this: "*God helps those who cannot help themselves.*" How does He "assist?" He can assist with His mighty arm, certainly, and is known to do so. But He also uses you and I to do His bidding through the ministry of *helps*.

The Word of God makes it absolutely clear that people are not self-sufficient, but require help from beyond themselves.

> He who trusts in his own heart is a fool.
>
> —Proverbs 28:26 NASB

> Apart from me you can do nothing.
>
> —John 15:5

> Our help is in the name of the Lord, who made heaven and earth.
>
> —Psalm 124:8

Knowing you have been made a new creation in Christ Jesus, *helps* is the outworking of your Christian identity. Jesus sent the Holy Spirit to all believers with gifts to be put to use for His service. As you allow this ministry of *helps* to work through you, not only will it serve others but you will increase the quality of your own spiritual life. You will discover your prayers more effective.

You will enjoy even more precious fellowship with your Savior. Not only will you be a blessing to others, but God will, in turn, bless you with abundance. As the Holy Spirit is the *helper* and that same Holy Spirit resides in you, there are no excuses. Our prospects are as bright as the promises of God. Your talent is God's gift to you. What you do with that talent is your gift back to God.

Remember, your gift of helps is a charisma, a gift God has given you through the Holy Spirit. As any gift of God, like the Word itself, *helps* is alive, overflowing with the life of God.

Though the New Testament offers example after example of *helps*, this ministry is recorded from the very first pages of scripture. The first mention of the word *help* (Hebrew *ezer*, עזר) is found in Genesis 2. "And the LORD God said, it is not good that the man should be alone; I will make him an help meet for him."[3] That is, "I will make a help suitable or sufficient for him." The transition from something that was "not good" to something "good" was made possible with *helps*.

Though Moses spoke to God and led his people out of Egypt to the Promised Land by the power or God, he too needed this powerful ministry of *helps*.

---

3 Genesis 2:18 KJV

> So, it came about when Moses held his hand up, that Israel prevailed, and when he let his hand down, Amalek prevailed. But Moses' hands were heavy. Then they took a stone and put it under him, and he sat on it; and Aaron and Hur supported his hands, one on one side and one on the other. Thus, his hands were steady until the sun set.
>
> —Exodus 17:11-12 NASB

In Exodus 18:4, Moses named one of his sons Eliezer, which means "God is help." In his farewell address to the children of Israel, Moses offered the following blessing.

> Blessed are you, O Israel: Who is like you, a people saved by the LORD? He is your shield and helper and your glorious sword. Your enemies will cower before you, and you will trample down their high places.
>
> —Deuteronomy 33:29 NIV

Though the gift of helps may appear no different than help offered from the non-believer, there is a significant difference between the two: one is empowered of the Holy Spirit, the other is not. The individual operating in the gift has an impact in the natural, certainly, and by obedience to the

Holy Spirit there is impact in the spiritual as well. In Exodus 17 Aaron and Hur held up the arms of Moses and the people of God prevailed, a physical act of *helps* with both a spiritual and supernatural effect.

THE PURPOSE OF HELPS

Ministry gifts are used to glorify Christ as Lord and to work out His purpose. They are spiritual, not natural, and take precedence and priority over every natural gift in our service to our Lord and as members of the body of Christ. This means that natural talent without a spiritual gift is inadequate for the fulfilment of the purposes God has called us to.

Acts 27 tells the story of a journey by ship with the Apostle Paul and Luke on board. Verse 14 says the wind was so strong and boisterous that it was difficult to maintain control of the ship. The wind is given the name *Euroclydon* (GK. ευροκλυδον), a tempest so robust that verses 17-19 say:

> When they had taken up, they used helps, undergirding the ship; and, fearing lest they should fall into the quicksands, strake sail, and so were driven. And we being exceedingly tossed with a tempest, the next day they light-

> ened the ship; And the third day we cast out with our own hands the tackling of the ship.
>
> —Acts 27:17-19 KJV

Note verse 17 uses the word *helps*. At that time, for a ship of the size in question, there would have been on board up to four seamen trained to do a very necessary but dangerous task. In a storm, with a rope tied around their waist, two of the seamen would dive overboard into the raging sea from each side of the boat, meet each other underneath the boat, and tie the ropes to secure the ship's planks that were in danger of being parted by the ferocity of the storm. This procedure, known as frapping, prevented the boat from sinking and causing great loss of life. There were two hundred and seventy-six onboard the ship in Acts 27. From the message the angel gave and Paul's confirmation,[4] we know that none were lost and the *helps* contribution was crucial. How many brothers and sisters in Christ are you undergirding with your gift of helps?

The application of the Holy Spirit's gift of helps may not be as dramatic as those on board the ship in Acts 27, but they nevertheless serve the same God, the God who overruled the captain's unbelief in the face of what appeared to be an impossible

---

4 Acts 27:22

situation (v. 44), thus averting catastrophe. None of the *helps* are identified by name, but they matter, and are known to God. He not only saw what they did, but strengthened, enabled, and caused them to be effective in their life-saving mission. When God calls you to be His *helps* in time of trouble He will equip you for the task He calls you to do.

> In the day of my trouble I call upon you, for you answer me.
>
> —PSALMS 86:7

The *helps* God used in ACTS 27:17, including the angel in v. 23-24, are unnamed. The scriptures are replete with people who did great things but remained anonymous. What matters is not earthly recognition, but that they were and forever will be known in heaven.

We don't know the names of all those who built the ark, the tabernacle, or the temple. They may remain unnamed, untrumpeted, and more than likely unappreciated, at least here on earth. Like many other kinds of *helps*, their numbers may remain unmeasurable, but those numbers will swell in heaven. They may be anonymous, but their deeds, that is, their acts of *helps*, are recorded in scripture. There are others—the boy who gave his lunch to Jesus to feed the five thousand,[5] the four helpers who lowered the sick man through a roof so that Jesus might heal him,[6] the lender of the colt that Jesus rode on his entrance to Jerusalem,[7] the lender of the upper room,[8] and the one who offered Jesus the sponge while He was on the cross.[9] And that is just a start.

Wise men came to see the baby Jesus and brought gifts, one of which was gold. It was God's provision for Mary and Joseph and their baby son Jesus for their flight to Egypt, and to keep them safe until they were able to return. This generosity by a foreign prince was an example of *helps*. We can see God in operation. His resources are inexhaustible. He owns the cattle on a thousand hills (and they're all debt free). He gives according to His riches. Wow! What you do may go unnoticed, but in enriching the lives of many, in exercising this gift, you will be accumulating a tax-free reward in heaven.

The fruit of *helps* is blessedness, generous and abundant, a blessedness that touches not only the one being helped, but the helper. You just can't bless someone without being blessed in return.

---

5 Mark 6:38

6 Luke 5:18

7 Matthew 21:3

8 Matthew 26:18

9 Matthew 27:48

The very act overflows with blessedness. And like someone standing close to a fire will be warmed, those who witness an act of *helps* cannot help but be blessed. Salvation has a reach that stretches far and wide.

> God has given us two hands, one to receive with and the other to give with.
>
> —Billy Graham

Faith in action is the fuel for a full life. I encourage you to start today. Ask the Holy Spirit to lead you. There are many who need your specific variety of *helps*. Yes, yours. As our eternal home becomes more real to us, we will pay more attention to applying our gift of helps, as it prepares us for our heavenly service.

Hebrews 2:16 reminds us, "For surely it is not angels He helps, but Abraham's descendants." That's us, you and me. Angels, however, are vital *helps* in our lives, unseen or unrecognized as they may be. There are two-hundred-and-ninety-eight references to the ministry of angels (divine *helps*) in thirty-four of the sixty-six books of the Bible. God's angels are available to assist us, in addition to the work of the Holy Spirit, in the administration of our gift of helps. Ask your Heavenly Father for assistance in times of need; His angels are innumerable to carry out His slightest bidding—I have experienced many such interventions by angels, and scripture confirms it:

> For he will command his angels concerning you to guard you in all your ways. On their hands they will bear you up, lest you strike your foot against a stone.
>
> —Psalm 91:11-12

Philippians 2:4 says, "Look not every man on his own things, but every man also on the things of others." By exercising the gift of helps we are in the ministry of *helps*. To help fallen members of the body of Christ, to defend our brothers and sisters when they are attacked, to apply the balm of Gilead, to be "fellow helpers to the truth."[10] When we do God's work in building His Kingdom, He helps us.[11] And the world will take notice.

Help those who can't help back.
Share the credit for your *helps*.
Determine to be a *helps* not a hindrance.

You could change the course of history through the power of the Holy Spirit—one life, a community, or even a whole nation. The ministry of Jesus

---

10 3 John 1:6

11 Nehemiah 6:16

is the model of *helps*. If you follow His example, and you are empowered by the Holy Spirit, you can not only make a difference, you can be the difference.

Chapter 2

ENCOURAGING

Therefore encourage one another and build one another up, just as you are doing.

—1 THESSALONIANS 5:11

. . . that their hearts may be encouraged, being knit together in love."

—COLOSSIANS 2:2

ENCOURAGEMENT is not only one of the most necessary of *helps*, it may be the easiest to exercise. Good investments go a long way and words are currency. What you do with that currency, how you choose to invest it, comes with responsibility. The next kind word you speak could change someone's afternoon, or state of mind, or entire life. Words can ignite action. They can initiate healing. Our words can make someone feel large, empowered, secure, capable of standing against any obstacle. They can also tear down and destroy, and with frighteningly little effort. Given we most often encourage by what we say, a brief reminder on words, their importance, and how to use them will be helpful.

According to PROVERBS 25:11, apt, well-chosen words are like "apples of gold in settings of silver." But choosing the "right" word is not as simple as it sounds. The power of the tongue is a continuous theme in scripture. It is clearly imperative to God that we understand its importance. With our tongue we confess. We bless. We instruct. With our tongue we also curse, tear down and ridicule. "The tongue is a fire," James says, "a world of evil . . . no man can tame the tongue."[12] To bring the tongue into submission, therefore, is impossible without divine intervention, or divine *helps*. Here are a few scriptures to consider regarding the power of our words:

> The tongue that brings healing is a tree of life,
> but a deceitful tongue crushes the spirit.
>
> —PROVERBS 15:4 NIV

12 JAMES 3:6 NIV

> Pleasant words are a honeycomb, sweet to the soul and healing to the bones.
>
> — Proverbs 16:24 NIV

> Pray also for me, that whenever I open my mouth, words may be given me so that I will fearlessly make known the mystery of the gospel.
>
> —Ephesians 6:19, NIV

> The wise in heart are called discerning, and pleasant words promote instruction.
>
> —Proverbs 16:21 NIV

The more we cultivate righteousness in our lives, the more our words reflect that righteousness. The more we feed upon the holy, the more the holy is reflected in our speech. The response becomes natural to the tongue, as one well practiced, taking orders as it does from a heart under command, thus enabling us to build each other up.

Feed on the Word. The more you feed on the Word, the more it cultivates you, that is, the more it prepares the tongue and the heart to exercise the "best" that is in you, with language that has more the soul of the builder than the demolition crew.

Joshua was a prince among men. His charge to the people is one of the better examples of encouragement in scripture. It projects fearlessness and unwavering confidence, with the strength and integrity of a command.

> Be strong and courageous, do not be frightened and do not be dismayed, for the LORD your God is with you wherever you go.
>
> —Joshua 1:9

A call to courage is a call to put fear in its rightful place, to put fear under restraints, and allow it no access to the will or the imagination. The prefix "en" means *within, inside.* To *en*-courage, therefore, is to speak courage *into* someone, to build them up in faith, to apply backbone to resolve, to speak fear *away from* them, that their way be clear, unobstructed, without distraction or hesitation—courage is fear prayed away. Joshua, who, time and again proved himself strong and courageous, spoke from his confidence (as courage does). "Be strong and courageous," he says, because the Lord "is with you wherever you go." You can trust his words. He speaks with certitude, knowing what he is sure of. It is the solid ground he stands on.

> In God I have put my trust, I shall not be afraid. What can man do to me?
>
> —Psalm 56:11 NASB

> The LORD is my light and my salvation; whom shall I fear? the LORD is the strength of my life; of whom shall I be afraid?
>
> —Psalm 21:1 NASB

The above passages say the same things in different ways, that is, they agree, they are informed by God and His will. There is consensus. I don't have to depend on my own strength. I can depend on the Lord, who is the strength of my life. Having appetite for the Word, and feeding on it regularly, the words Joshua speaks are full of life, full of agreement with God, and, in essence, full of God.

"Let there be light," God said. Creation was in his speech, in words specifically chosen, Spirit-breathed and appointed. That same creative spirit lives in our speech. That is one reason it is impossible to tame. Here is a short review of what words are capable of:

> *They build. They tear down.*
> *They imagine. They doubt.*
> *They roar. They bleat.*
> *They heal. They injure.*
> *They curse. They bless.*
> *They howl. They praise.*

SUBSTANCE, NOT WIND

Scripture warns that, "*Death and life are in the power of the tongue, And those who love it will eat its fruit.*"[13] The tongue is our most conspicuous organ; lamentably, it is most often our first defense; it gets us in the most trouble at times; it is ever too willing to draw attention to itself; and scripture refers to the tongue as a "fire" (and that's not always a good thing). Unsurprisingly therefore, it often takes supernatural intervention to restrain it and put it to good use.

Encouragement is set in motion and accomplished most often by words, words with substance, not wind, words that mean what they say when they say it, that speak to individual need, words that encourage, that invite others to hope, that help them understand and see how beautiful, how necessary, and what healing they can do. Encouragement is an investment to make and to watch prosper.

In the ministry of *helps*, if we are dedicated, if we are sincere, if we pray a prayer of submission to God, if we rest in His wisdom, the words we speak are chosen for us. They come naturally to us, or as one who has been taught well and governed well. The following passages were trusted to servants like Peter, Paul, Isaiah, and David the King.

---

13 Proverbs 18:21 NAS

Casting all your anxieties on him, because he cares for you.

—1 Peter 5:7

Therefore encourage one another with these words.

—1 Thessalonians 4:18

When you pass through the waters I will be with you; and through the rivers, they shall not overwhelm you.

—Isaiah 43:2

Be strong and let your heart take courage, all you who wait for the LORD.

—Psalm 31:24

That through the encouragement of the scriptures we might have hope.

—Romans 15:4

WHILE WAITING FOR THE WORLD TO COME

In the heart of any word or any action empowered by or set in motion by God, is the knowledge that this world is not our home. The righteousness we live by and communicate in this world is in preparation for a new one. It is a language and a code we seek among us, a new tongue, the way of heaven, the language of our homeland. We are told in 2 Peter 3:12 ESV that we are "*waiting for new heavens and a new earth in which righteousness dwells.*" So, vital to encouragement is to share the hope of glory that we have as we await the return of our blessed Lord who could come back for the church at any time. Encouraging words are empowered to keep us on track and moving forward, as we await His return.

A kind word in a moment of need is the language of heaven both to the one who hears it and the one who speaks. The language of heaven should be familiar to us, particularly if we exercise it regularly—the warmth, the selflessness, the authentic love and care invested in each syllable. It will be seasoned with hope and irrevocable good will. Heaven should be a familiar place. We should be able to detect the language when we hear it, and not just from the scripture but from close listening to one another. By exercising the gift of helps, we bring heaven closer, so close in fact that our language is animated with it, brightened by it, alive and full of hope.

My late brother, Adrian, led me to the Lord when he was fifteen and I was thirteen. He continually encouraged me and helped me to study the Word. He died when he was twenty-three, leaving behind two sons under three years old. It was a huge loss in my life, but I am part of what he left behind, part of his legacy, a return on what he invested in me. He used the following passages to encourage me, just before he went to be with his Lord.

When you say: It is impossible.
God says: All things are possible.

—LUKE 18:27

When you say: I'm too tired.
God says: I will give you rest.

—MATTHEW 11:28-30

When you say: Nobody really loves me.
God says: I love you.

—JOHN 3:16

When you say: I can't go on.
God says: My grace is sufficient.

—2 CORINTHIANS 12:19

When you say: I can't figure things out.
God says: I will direct your steps.

—PROVERBS 3:6

When you say: I can't do it.
God says: You can do all things.

—PHILIPPIANS 4:13

When you say: I'm not able.
God says: I am able.

—2 CORINTHIANS 9:8

When you say: It's not worth it.
God says: It will be worth it.

—ROMANS 8:28

When you say: I can't forgive myself.
God says: I forgive you.

—1 JOHN 1:9

When you say: I'm afraid.
God says: I have not given you the spirit of fear.

—2 TIMOTHY 1:7

When you say: I'm always worried and frustrated.
God says: Cast all your cares on me.

—1 PETER 5:7

When you say: I'm not smart enough.
God says: I will give you wisdom.

—1 CORINTHIANS 1:3

When you say: I feel all alone.
God says: I will never leave you nor forsake you.

—HEBREWS 13:5

When you say: I can't manage.
God says: I will supply all your needs.

—PHILIPPIANS 4:19

When you say: Help, Lord.
God says: Do not fear; I will help you.

—ISAIAH 41:13

YOU CAN'T HAVE A RAINBOW WITHOUT RAIN

If we remind ourselves daily of the promises of God, we will be more able to impart that same encouragement to others. God has not promised sun without rain, joy without sorrow, peace without pain, but He has promised strength for the day, rest for the laborer, light on the way, grace for the trials, help from above, unfailing sympathy, undying love, and *helps* from the body of Christ. We can be assured that the will of God will never take us where the grace of God will not protect us, so our work is to cast away care, while God's work is to take on that care. In His divine discernment, God chooses what we go through. It is however our choice as to how we go through it.

You can't have a rainbow without rain. The rainbow is the visible manifestation of a promise of God and cannot occur without rain. As believers we should be the rainbow to the tears of others, as we exercise the gift of helps by encouraging them that the God who made the rainbow, will do the same by His Holy Spirit. Consider the following passages:

> For this light momentary affliction is preparing for us an eternal weight of glory beyond all comparison.
>
> —2 Corinthians 4:17

> It is the LORD who goes before you. He will be with you; he will not leave you or forsake you. Do not fear or be dismayed.
>
> —Deuteronomy 31:8

> Everything is possible for one who believes.
>
> —Mark 9:23 NIV

There was an apostle named Joseph, who demonstrated the gift of helps in a number of ways. He was clearly a wealthy individual. In Acts 4:34, following a powerful filling of the Holy Spirit we are told, "There was not a needy person among them, for as many as were owners of lands or houses sold them and brought the proceeds of what was sold." One of the people that sold property to contribute to the collective was Joseph. You may wonder why you haven't heard of this "Joseph" before. That is because he is more often known by the name the apostles gave him, *Barnabas*, which means "son of encouragement."[14]

Barnabas lived out the spirit of his name with great effect. He was an incredible example of the gift of helps, taking Saul (who became Paul) under his wing and supporting him, as well as later advocating for John-Mark to be given a second chance

---

14 Acts 4:36

in ministry after he had deserted Paul and Barnabas earlier. Barnabas provided great *helps* to the Apostle Paul, along with Timothy who would become his successor. What about in your life? Are there those in ministry who you can encourage? Who has God put in your path to bless with your gift of *helps*? It may be that a brother or sister in the Lord needs your gift of helps, expressed through words of encouragement to lift them up during the trials they are facing.

Charles Spurgeon, speaking on 1 Peter 5:7, writes encouragingly, "His heart beats with pity for your woe and His hand omnipotent shall yet bring you the needed help."[15] Spurgeon then reminds us of Hebrews 13:5 KJV, "I will never leave thee, nor forsake thee." In this promise, God gives to His people everything. God is love, so with loving-kindness He will have mercy upon us. He said, "My grace is sufficient for you."[16] If, as believers, we are not tried and tested, we cannot give the testimony of the solace we have found in His divine grace. But we can rest assured that the God who has met our needs until now can be trusted to the end of our days.

Pray with me. *By thy power, O blessed Holy Spirit, may my heart rejoice in the truth that for*

---

15 Charles Haddon Spurgeon, Devotions (Morning) of C. H. Spurgeon, Public Domain.

16 2 Corinthians 12:9

me to live is Christ and to die is even more Christ for all eternity.

LET US HOLD FAST

In the spring of 1980, I attended the first African Heads of State Prayer Breakfast in Monrovia, Liberia. The country was the chair country that year of the *Organization of African Unity*. Eleven heads of state attended. Hosted by the President, Dr. Tolbert (a former Baptist pastor) and attended by his wife, Victoria. I represented the fellowship of believers from Great Britain and was surprised by the Word the Holy Spirit laid on my heart to share.

> Let us draw near with a sincere heart in full assurance of faith, having our hearts sprinkled clean from an evil conscience and our bodies washed with pure water. Let us hold fast the confession of our hope without wavering, for He who promised is faithful; and let us consider how to stimulate one another to love and good deeds . . .
>
> —Hebrews 10:22-24 NASB

Three simple thoughts: *draw near, hold fast*, and *consider*. I preached what I was meant to preach, what the Lord had put on my heart. Later that day, I left for the airport to return to London. Arriving the following morning, I was met off the plane and asked when I had last been with President Tolbert. I explained I had said my goodbye earlier in the afternoon, gone straight to the airport and now was back in London. I was then told, to my complete shock, that after my departure there had been a violent military coup in Liberia, and that President Tolbert had been beheaded. To add to the horror, his wife, Victoria, had been stripped naked, marched around the city square, and shown where they had thrown her husband's head. Their daughter, Christina, had been thrown in prison and most of the cabinet had been killed. I could not have been more shocked and saddened by this news.

Five weeks later, I received in my mail a torn piece of brown paper from what had been a large, brown envelope. On one side was my name and address and a postage stamp from Liberia. On the other side was hand written and smuggled out of her prison cell the words, "let us draw near, let us hold fast, let us consider one another." To these words were added, "Thank you for being obedient to the Holy Spirit's leading. Your message has been my daily strength. Thank you for your faithfulness. God's will *will* be done." This message had come from the President and First Lady's daughter, Christina.

Sometime after that, we were able to arrange for her to leave the country, but I was humbled to be encouraged by someone whose circumstances had been so unimaginable. She encouraged me, even as God had encouraged her through my obedience.

There is no better place for us to turn for encouragement than the Word of God. One of my favorite places to turn to in Scripture is PSALM 23, and the following twelve truths from this Psalm offer encouragement of a sublime nature. Because God is "perfect," His words are charged by His Spirit and overflow with His perfection, and so I make no apology for including the encouraging words below in most all of my writings.

I shall not want (v. 1)
Perfect salvation.

He makes me lie down in green pastures (v. 2)
Perfect rest.

He leads me beside still waters (v. 2)
Perfect refreshment.

He restores my soul (v. 3)
Perfect recovery.

He leads me in paths of righteousness (v. 3)
Perfect guidance.

I will fear no evil (v. 4)
Perfect protection.

You are with me (v. 4)
Perfect company.

You prepare a table (v. 5)
Perfect provision.

You anoint my head (v. 5)
Perfect consecration.

My cup overflows (v. 5)
Perfect joy.

Goodness and mercy shall follow me (v. 6)
Perfect care.

I shall dwell in the house of the Lord forever (v. 6)
Perfect destiny.

An unknown author wrote, "I should have been proud to hold the spy-glass for Columbus, to have picked up the fallen brush for Michelangelo, to have carried Milton's bag, or to have blown the organ bellows for Handel." Similarly, many of us may wish we could have walked with the Lord and ministered to Him as Mary Magdalene did, or to have walked the Emmaus Road as Cleopas did with Jesus on the day of His resurrection. (Luke 24). We can. We all can. You and I can, today, by living in the fullness of our gift of helps to and for others, and so have the joy of hearing in our spirit, "Truly, I say to you, as you did it to one of the least of these my brothers, you did it to me."[17]

O God, our Help in ages past,
our Hope for years to come,
Be Thou our Guide while life shall last,
and our eternal Home.

—Isaac Watts
"O God, Our Help In Ages Past"

17 Matthew 25:40

Chapter 3

LOVING

This is my commandment, that you love one another as I have loved you.

—John 15:12

And the King will answer them, "Truly, I say to you, as you did it to one of the least of these my brothers, you did it to me."

—Matthew 25:40

The gift of helps assists those in need. There is not a clearer definition of *helps* than that. There are many levels of need. There are immediate needs—hunger, lodging, financial support, and similar needs which are close to the surface. If someone is hungry, you feed them. If someone is in need of encouragement, you offer a kind word. And so on. There are also needs of a deeper nature, most often hidden below the surfaces of life. Helping someone at those levels demands greater personal investment. But whether offering help in great or small ways, there is one element common to all, something at the heart of *helps* that gives it life and vibrancy, which springs from the very soul of the Gospel. That common element is love. Just as this chapter is at the center of this little book, so love lies at the heart and soul of *helps*. Love is the fuel that drives it, that moves it forward.

You can give without loving, but you cannot love without giving and sharing with those in need. The gift of helps is based on this common scriptural theme, *loving our neighbor as ourselves.*[18] I am a debtor to my neighbor as if he or she were Christ himself, and so if my possessions belong to Christ, then my neighbor should have access to them where they have need, with the same rights as Christ does.

The gift of helps is a biblically based gift of the Holy Spirit, given to the body of Christ as a manifestation that we are children of God living out the love that is within us by lovingly helping others

---

18 Mark 12:31

both inside the church and outside. It is a helping hand, a listening ear, a loving word in season. It is not only helping with the chores, and other small duties, but it implies the availability and willingness to do extra, to go beyond the basics and what is asked. True Christ-like love in action, regardless of who sees it. Sometimes charity is noticed. Just as often it is not. Either way, what is accomplished in love, what is done out of sheer joy and obedience to Christ, is considered "well done" in God's estimation, as in "Well done, thou good and faithful servant."[19]

> But love your enemies, and do good, and lend, expecting nothing in return, and your reward will be great, and you will be sons of the Most High, for he is kind to the ungrateful and the evil.
>
> —Luke 6:35

We have seen that the gift of helps is a special gift of showing the love of God to others. But we can also see that it is not only about showing the love of God to others by our service, but it is a way of loving God himself. Loving our neighbor *is* loving God. Serving our neighbor in love *is* serving God. There are many people who seem tireless at

---

19 Matthew 25:21 KJV

helping others and are really energized by it. The use of the gift of helps is clear evidence of the Gospel within us. It is eager to express itself because God's love inspires us to serve in love and cultivate a spirit of love and kindness toward one another. In this spirit, it is truly "more blessed to give than to receive."[20]

> He has told you, O man, what is good; and what does the LORD require of you but to do justice, and to love kindness, and to walk humbly with your God?
>
> —Micah 6:8

NO LIMITS

There was a time when it appeared that God failed to help His own Son. When Jesus cried out from the cross, "My God, my God, why have you forsaken me?"[21] He fulfilled prophecy from Psalm 22. God forsook His Son so that we would never be forsaken. It was because of the sacrifice of Jesus on our behalf and His "helplessness" that we are able to say by faith that the eternal God is our help.

20 Acts 20:35

21 Matthew 27:46

He will never leave me nor forsake me. His love has no limits, His grace no measure, His power no boundary known to man. For out of His infinite riches in Jesus He giveth, and giveth and giveth again. "Through the love of God, our Savior, all will be well."[22]

The second principal command of scripture, is "love your neighbor as yourself"[23]. A core foundation of the entire canon of scripture from Genesis to Revelation, this is integral to the application of the gift of helps. 1 THESSALONIANS 3:12 ESV says, "abound in love for one another." It is because of the love poured out for us on the cross of Calvary that we are compelled to love one another, not only helping those in need but demonstrating to the world that we are Jesus' disciples.

> I thank my God always when I remember you in my prayers, because I hear of your love and of the faith that you have toward the Lord Jesus and for all the saints.
>
> —PHILEMON 1:4-5

Empowered by the Holy Spirit, *helps* is the gift of love that knows no boundaries. It is the love that shares, that gives of itself joyfully and com-

---

22 MARY B. PETERS, "THROUGH THE LOVE OF GOD OUR SAVIOUR," 1847.

23 MARK 12:31

pletely. Just as Jesus gave himself for us, taking up our pain and bearing our suffering; now it is our turn to imitate Christ, to ease what suffering we can, to share the burdens and needs of others out of our thankfulness for who we are in Christ.

> Oh help me understand it,
> help me to take it in,
> what it meant to thee the holy one
> to bear away my sin.
>
> —K. A. M. Kelly
> "Give Me A Sight, O Savior"

Dietrich Bonhoeffer put it this way, "only a suffering God can help." We are to exercise the gifts we are given, to love and serve others. I asked a dear friend, Dr. Jack Graham, Pastor of Prestonwood Baptist Church, Texas, to share with me his observation on the gift of helps. Not surprisingly, he referenced scripture, responding that, "it is the same as the gift of service in Romans 12:7 or similar, supporting the work of the church in practical ways in order to meet the needs of others." Below is the entire passage from Romans 12 on the character of ministry, and the love at its core.

> 6 Since we have gifts that differ according to the grace given to us, each of us is to exercise them

accordingly: if prophecy, according to the pro-
portion of his faith; [7] if service, in his serving;
or he who teaches, in his teaching; [8] or he who
exhorts, in his exhortation; he who gives, with
liberality; he who leads, with diligence; he who
shows mercy, with cheerfulness.

[9] Let love be without hypocrisy. Abhor what
is evil; cling to what is good. [10] Be devoted to
one another in brotherly love; give preference
to one another in honor; [11] not lagging behind
in diligence, fervent in spirit, serving the Lord;
[12] rejoicing in hope, persevering in tribulation,
devoted to prayer, [13] contributing to the needs
of the saints, practicing hospitality.

[14] Bless those who persecute you; bless and
do not curse. [15] Rejoice with those who re-
joice, and weep with those who weep. [16] Be of
the same mind toward one another; do not be
haughty in mind, but associate with the lowly.
Do not be wise in your own estimation. [17] Never
pay back evil for evil to anyone. Respect what
is right in the sight of all men. [18] If possible, so
far as it depends on you, be at peace with all
men. [19] Never take your own revenge, beloved,
but leave room for the wrath of God, for it is
written, "VENGEANCE IS MINE, I WILL REPAY,"
says the Lord. [20] "BUT IF YOUR ENEMY IS HUN-
GRY, FEED HIM, AND IF HE IS THIRSTY, GIVE HIM

> A DRINK; FOR IN SO DOING YOU WILL HEAP BURNING COALS ON HIS HEAD." [21] Do not be overcome by evil, but overcome evil with good.
>
> —ROMANS 12:6-21 NASB

The Word teaches us that *love should be without suppression,* that it may be the first and deepest response in us, so that Christ is free to live, move, and have His being in us (Acts 17:28), that His life may be shared and the blessing be bountiful and unending. These words must surely motivate all true believers to help others out of love. "We have freely received, so we should freely give."[24] We read in HEBREWS 6:10 ESV, "For God is not unjust so as to overlook your work and the love that you have shown for his name in serving the saints, as you still do." He assures us that He will reward us in due season for the love we have shared. So we see that the gift of helps meets needs in a practical way, for we become even what non-believers call "a godsend," the love of Jesus in action.

> May the Lord direct your hearts to the love of God and to the steadfastness of Christ.
>
> —2 THESSALONIANS 3:5

---

24 MATTHEW 10:8

Jesus showed love from the cradle to the cross, where He laid down His life for you and for me, as He who knew no sin, became sin. He rose from the dead, victor over death, the devil and the grave, ascended to His Father in Heaven in His glorified human body and then sent us His promised Holy Spirit. He returned to heaven to prepare a place for us and when we get there, we will see the print of the nails in his hands and feet—the only man-made thing that will be in heaven. I believe that the Word makes it clear that it would be a rejection of the gift of helps within us not to exercise it with a heart full of love, knowing the extravagant love He has shown us.

> We love because He first loved us.
>
> —1 John 3:19

> He has given us His Spirit.
>
> —1 John 3:13

> And this is love, that we walk after His commandments.
>
> —2 John 1:6

God loves His children unfathomably and unconditionally with His unmerited love—there is no love like the love of Jesus, a love that goes the distance. "So now faith, hope, and love abide, these three; but the greatest of these is love."[25] The gift that only God could give out of His love for us was His Son, Jesus. Therefore, as we have received this love which has no limits, so we can now give it to others without conditions or expectations.

> I will recount the steadfast love of the LORD, the praises of the LORD, according to all that the LORD has granted us, and the great goodness to the house of Israel that he has granted them according to his compassion, according to the abundance of his steadfast love.
>
> —Isaiah 63:7

All believers are called to help others as unto the Lord, not unto man, and this pleases God. Galatians 5:22-23 says, "But the fruit of the Spirit is love, joy, peace, patience, kindness, goodness, faithfulness, gentleness, self-control." If we say we are filled with the Holy Spirit, we must bear evidence of His fruits. Our Lord called us to abide in Him and in His love. "And he who loves me will be loved by my Father, and I will love him and manifest myself to him."[26] We sing,

---

25 1 Corinthians 13:13

26 John 14:21

Now none but Christ can satisfy,
None other name for me;
There's love and life and lasting joy,
Lord Jesus, found in Thee.

—Emma Frances Shuttleworth Bevan
"O Christ In Thee My Soul Hath Found"

In 1999, in aid of the British Red Cross during the appalling Kosovo War, I published a book called My Favourite Hymn, which asked one hundred famous people in Great Britain what their favorite hymn was and why. The idea for this book came from a chance remark during a conversation I had with Dr. Billy Graham a few years earlier, when Dr. Graham observed that the majority of people today learn their initial theology from hymns. That was enough to inspire me to compile the book.

One of the contributors to My Favourite Hymn was Baroness Margaret Thatcher, who was the British Prime Minister for ten years. When I asked her for her favorite hymn, without hesitation she said, "Jesus, Lover Of My Soul," by Charles Wesley. I asked why it was her favorite. "Although the great Hymns of Praise and their marvelous tunes crowd into one's mind immediately," she said, "I have chosen 'Jesus, Lover Of My Soul' sung to the tune 'Aberystwyth' because it concerns one's personal relationship with God, especially when times are difficult. Then these lovely words and this particular tune bring comfort and calm to the troubled mind."

Jesus, lover of my soul,
Let me to Thy bosom fly,
While the nearer waters roll,
While the tempest still is high.
Hide me, O my Savior, hide,
Till the storm of life is past;
Safe into the haven guide;
Oh, receive my soul at last.

Other refuge have I none,
Hangs my helpless soul on Thee;
Leave, ah! leave me not alone,
Still support and comfort me.
All my trust on Thee is stayed,
All my help from Thee I bring;
Cover my defenseless head
With the shadow of Thy wing.

—Charles Wesley
"Jesus, Lover Of My Soul"

As Baroness Thatcher intimated with her hymn choice, love is the anthem of our homeland, where the Father's heart is most glorified through us. It cannot help but sing out from us as we continue to live and move and have our being in Him, building ourselves up in His love.

> But you, beloved, building yourselves up in your most holy faith and praying in the Holy Spirit, keep yourselves in the love of God, waiting for the mercy of our Lord Jesus Christ that leads to eternal life.
>
> —JUDE 1:20-21

Chapter 4

PRAYING

Pray without ceasing.

—1 THESSALONIANS 5:17 NKJV

Confess your trespasses to one another, and pray for one another, that you may be healed. The effective, fervent prayer of a righteous man avails much.

—JAMES 5:16 NKJV

WITHOUT PRAYER, WE CAN DO NOTHING. Without prayer, we *should* do nothing. With prayer, HEBREWS 4:17 tells us, "we will find grace to help in time of need." Prayer changes things. It should therefore preface everything we undertake. It moves the heart of God. It orders the heart of man. You could be the answer to someone's cry for help. The power of prayer does not depend on the one who prays, but on the one who hears, our Lord and Savior Jesus Christ. Our prayers matter in heaven and we do well to remember that any seeming delay in our prayers being answered, is not denial—God's timing is perfect.

One of the greatest gifts we can offer to our fellow brothers and sisters is prayer on their behalf. For the strength to endure the spiritual warfare we inevitably face, the Apostle Paul tells us to pray "at all times in the Spirit, with all prayer and supplication. To that end, keep alert with all perseverance, making supplication for all the saints."[27]

The gift of helps, expressed through prayer, is a significant aid for others in their times of trial and tribulation. Alongside offering practical support where needed, let us also offer our gift of helps in prayer for those in need of spiritual breakthrough. To intercede is to stand in the gap for someone else. Our Lord Jesus Christ is the great intercessor, who offered Himself as a propitiation for our sins,[28] and who intercedes for us at the right hand of the Father.[29] Again, imitating Christ, we have

---

27 Ephesians 6:18

28 1 John 2:2

29 Romans 8:34

the privilege of interceding on behalf of our brothers and sisters in Him. Perhaps the most needed element of your gift of helps is to stand in prayer for those who cannot stand or kneel alone, especially when we remember that no one stands any higher than when on their knees before the Lord.

> I have been driven many times upon my knees by the overwhelming conviction that I had nowhere else to go. My own wisdom and that of all about me seemed insufficient for that day.
>
> —Abraham Lincoln

AGREEMENT: COVENANT PRAYER

> Again I say to you that if two of you agree on earth concerning anything that they ask, it will be done for them by My Father in heaven. For where two or three are gathered together in My name, I am there in the midst of them.
>
> —Matthew 18:19-20 NKJV

The Bible is clear that we have a strong weapon—covenant prayer. Now that you've read the above scripture, I encourage you to print verse 19 (*if two of you agree*) on your mind, heart, soul, and spirit. These verses tell us there is no greater power than agreement. Our authority is infused and empowered by Christ in our agreement with Him. If you will join one other person in agreement concerning any good thing—the salvation of a loved one, healing, provision, direction—and you consistently pray in covenant, Jesus says it will be done. What a motivational encouragement for us to be on our knees in covenantal prayer.

The Word of God shows us the covenant principle here, that if two or three of us will commit to come together in agreement, once, twice or three times a day, in His name, by God's grace, it will come to pass. This is something we can all be part of. There are many "twos" in the body of Christ: husbands and wives, fathers and daughters, mothers and sons, aunts and uncles, grandparents and godparents, business colleagues and friends. For God's glory and for His name's sake, I would urge you to enter into a covenant commitment to pray with one other person, to see God fulfil His Word. Determine how you can use your gift of helps in this way, offering the strength of agreement in prayer. You will make a difference. Pray.

Trust Jesus at His Word in Matthew 18:19. In doing this, you will be fully blessed, and you will become a vessel to bless others. Indeed, prayer should be like breathing for a believer. It should be a natural response to all life sends in our direction, by kneeling before the throne of God and seeking His help. Jabez, in his prayer in 1 Chronicles 4:11, did not hesitate to ask God for four things.

1. That God would bless him.
2. That God would enlarge him.
3. That God would be with him.
4. That God would keep him.

God answered Jabez. We too can pray this prayer and see it answered. We serve a God that neither slumbers nor sleeps.[30] He listens 24/7, but even that is not saying enough. Given time loses its authority with God, He has an ear for us in and out of time. He is a sovereign God, creator of all things seen and unseen, the King of Kings and Lord of Lords, above all principalities, powers and authorities. His name is above every name. He is "a very present help in trouble."[31] Be encouraged, therefore. He is there for us, whenever we call on His name, whenever we seek Him in prayer, even when we don't know what to ask for: "For we do not know what to pray for as we ought, but the Spirit himself intercedes for us with groaning too deep for words."[32]

---

30 Psalm 121:4

31 Psalm 46:1

32 Romans 8:26

Prayer is the soul's sincere desire,
Uttered or unexpressed,
The motion of a hidden fire
That trembles in the breast.

Prayer is the burden of a sigh,
The falling of a tear,
The upwards glancing of an eye
When none but God is near.

Prayer is the Christian's vital breath,
The Christian's native air,
His watchword at the gates of death;
He enters Heav'n with prayer.

—James Montgomery
"Prayer is the soul's sincere desire"

What you pray today will determine how you live when you rise from your knees. Remember, you can't lose your footing when you're on your knees. Tears may fall, but prayers rise to the King of Kings. So, don't worry about anything and pray about everything. Let your prayers replace your worries and keep in mind that the distance between a problem and its solution is the distance of your knees from the floor. So, when life gets too hard to stand, just kneel and pray.

Our prayers do not need to be long. The creature cries out to the creator in Psalm 12:1 (King

David's shortest prayer), "Help, Lord." In David's need, he turns to his God and in faith pleads to the one who knows everything about him and his circumstances. He offers a "two-word" prayer to our triune God (Father, Son and Holy Spirit). David had a need and God had the answer. "When other helpers fail and comforts flee," the old hymn says, "*Help of the helpless, oh, abide with me.*"[33] The helpline to heaven, prayer, demonstrated by David, is still available to us continually. When we kneel in prayer, seeking heavenly help, God never ignores us.

Such was the impact of God's intervention in the life of His prophet Samuel that he took a stone, and set it between Mizpah and Shen and called the name of it Ebenezer, saying "Thus far the LORD has helped us."[34] Isaiah 41:14 NASB says, "'I will help you,' declares the LORD." It is biblical to say, as Job did, "Is not my help in me?"[35] When our best efforts are inadequate, we are driven to our knees by faith, to the throne of grace where reigns our all-sufficient Lord and Savior Jesus Christ, ready to help us in our time of need. Faith needs few words; our Savior intercedes on our behalf to His Father and

---

33 Henry Lyte, "Abide With Me"

34 1 Samuel 7:12 NASB

35 Job 6:13 KJV

ours. As we cry "help," Jesus says, "Fear not, I am the one who helps you."[36]

To enrich our prayer lives, we can do no better than to read our Lord's longest recorded prayer in John 17. In it, Jesus prays for protection, sanctification and unity for His disciples and all believers. I think it is the perfect prayer for our daily devotion and should precede our own prayers, as it sets a standard we would do well to emulate, in our praise and worship to the Father, Son and Holy Spirit.

As we offer our services in prayer for and with others in the body of Christ, we exercise our gift of helps through "helping prayer." By joining in covenant with others to see the promises of God fulfilled, we can then watch as the Holy Spirit empowers our gift of helps in ways we could not have imagined.

LET ME PRAY FOR YOU

I had returned from New York to London for the UK May holiday weekend and shall never forget how, on the morning of 5 May 1982, during a testing period in my life, heaven seemed closed. Mute even. Silent. Once dressed, I sat on the side of my bed and prayed, "Heavenly Father, I feel you've

---

36 Isaiah 41:13 ESV

left me, that you aren't hearing me, that you've abandoned me, and I've deserved it. But you say in your Word that you will never leave me, and never forsake me. Please would you give me a 'pin prick of light today,' that you haven't stopped loving me, that you still accept me, and I'll never stop praising you and giving testimony to it. Amen."

I put my jacket on, walked down the two flights of stairs to the ground floor where I had my office, and my long-standing receptionist, Jane, greeted me.

"Sir," she said, "Dr. Billy Graham called you."

"Well what does he want," I asked.

"Well," she said, "why don't we go into the office, I'll get him on the phone, and you can find out."

Her tone was sarcastic, and deservedly so, but nonetheless only served to scare me even further as to how far I was from where I should be. I walked into my office, the phone rang, I picked it up, and it was Billy's voice.

"Graham, I called to tell you something. I read about you in the *Wall Street Journal*, while flying here to Paris yesterday. I leave in one hour for my first visit to Russia. I have never been as sure before, as I am now, that the Lord loves you, because those the Lord loves He chastens and He's chastening you, Graham—He's going to purify you and make you the man that He has always planned and purposed for you to be. Can I pray with you?"

When you get a call like that, you don't say no, you say "yes please," and so I agreed. Billy prayed and when he'd finished, he said: "Can we meet three weeks from today, at 11 a.m. at the Essex House Hotel, Central Park South, New York?"

"By God's grace I will be there, Billy," I responded. It wasn't even a question of looking at my calendar. That was what I was going to do. It was agreed and then he was gone, to catch his flight. I put the phone down and the verse from Isaiah 65:24 (NKJV) came to me—

> It shall come to pass
> that before they call, I will answer;
> and while they are still speaking, I will hear.

While I was upstairs praying for a "pin prick" of light that God still loved me, Billy had already telephoned. Before I had finished praying, he'd left a message with Jane asking for me to call him within the hour as he was about to leave for Russia. While I was yet speaking, God answered.

That truth is as valid today as it was in 1982, for our God changes not. His YEA is YEA and His NAY is NAY. He loves us with His Father's heart and if

He loves me, as I know He does, He most surely can and does love you.

What Dr. Billy Graham took the time to do, with all that was on his mind and all he had on his very large plate, was an act of *helps*. It is an experience that I have frequently looked back on with a heart full of thankfulness toward Dr. Graham and my Heavenly Father for answered prayer.

> And this is the confidence that we have toward him, that if we ask anything according to his will he hears us. And if we know that he hears us in whatever we ask, we know that we have the requests that we have asked of him.
>
> —1 John 5:14-15

When it comes to prioritizing time to pray for our friends, Job is a great encouragement. This may surprise some, as Job's name is synonymous with suffering and persecution, but we read in Job 42:10,12 KJV that, "The LORD turned the captivity of Job, when he prayed for his friends: also the LORD gave Job twice as much as he had before... So the LORD blessed the latter days of Job more than his beginning." The turning point for Job came when he was on his knees, interceding for his friends. It is the intercessory prayer on behalf of others that is the key to being a blessing and being blessed ourselves.

You may also wish to encourage those you are praying for to join with you in praying for the greater needs of someone else as well, whether well known to you or because of some disaster in the world. Not only does this bring a promised blessing, but also a perspective in the light of the much greater needs of those we're praying for.

On the flip side, a recipe for misery is for us to think only of ourselves and not the needs of others. In fact, the best therapy for our own needs is having a concern for others and exercising our Holy Spirit gift of helps to be a blessing, by projecting the very blessing you desire for yourself onto others, with all the intensity and labor it may ask. Job had been overwhelmed, understandably, by the loss of his wife, family, home, wealth, health, and self-respect until he began to pray for others. All the time the Lord held the key to his release, relief and restitution from his bondage born out of extreme testing.

You cannot do more for yourself or others than pray, filling that space between you and someone in need with the life of God, for prayer is full of light and God's hidden wisdom.

Chapter 5

SHARING

Share with the Lord's people who are in need. Practice hospitality.

—Romans 12:13 NIV

Do not neglect to show hospitality to strangers, for thereby some have entertained angels unawares.

—Hebrews 13:2

Sharing and serving is love in action. So how do we share? What do we share? Why do we share? How do we share effectively?

Galatians 6:2 NLT says, "Share each other's burdens, and in this way obey the law of Christ."

It is said that a burden shared is a burden halved, that a word in season shared shows that you cared. The burdens we help carry and the words we share can have a profound impact on the lives of others, as we embrace the gift of helps by the power of the Holy Spirit. Romans 12:14 ESV says, "Rejoice with those who rejoice, weep with those who weep" and in Numbers 11:17 ESV when speaking to Moses, God says, "And I will take some of the Spirit that is on you and put it on them, and they shall bear the burden of the people with you, so that you may not bear it yourself alone."

The ministry of *helps* was given to us to be a blessing to the body of Christ and to witness to non-believers. As you help lift your brother or sister out of the darkest places through prayer and care, you will see them become all that God has called them and is preparing them to be. By sharing the burdens of those in ministry, the leaders and the pioneers, and lending your strength to the broken and the burnt-out, you can make a difference.

Sometimes we expect those in ministry leadership to do it all themselves, but the Apostles recognized that they needed all the help they could get:

> And the twelve summoned the full number of the disciples and said, 'It is not right that we

> should give up preaching the word of God to serve tables. Therefore, brothers, pick out from among you seven men of good repute, full of the Spirit and of wisdom, whom we will appoint to this duty. But we will devote ourselves to prayer and to the ministry of the word.'
>
> —Acts 6:2-4

How can you help your pastor or leader, so that they can focus their time and energy on the things God has called them to do?

The main thing we all have that we can share, is our life, which we can share as a member of the family of God. After all, Jesus shared Himself for you and me when He gave Himself up for us on the cross. He calls us to "be devoted to one another in brotherly love; [giving] preference to one another in honor."[37] How are you serving your life with others in love?

NOT A SENSATION, BUT A SERVANT

God has not saved you to be a sensation, but a servant. We are called to spread His Word as the Holy Spirit leads, to share the Gospel, that it might be said that you and I are "well reported for good

---

37 Romans 12:10 NASB

works,"[38] that we are "rich in good works, to be generous and ready to share, thus storing up treasure...as a good foundation for the future, so that they may take hold of that which is truly life."[39] Remain strong, with your eye on the prize, as scripture reminds us, "Be not be weary in well doing, for in due time we shall reap, if we faint not."[40]

The story of the Good Samaritan in LUKE 10:30-37 offers a demonstration of the gift of helps. We are encouraged to have the same heart attitude and actions toward our neighbor. The first question the priest and Levite most likely asked themselves was, "If I stop to help this man, what will happen to me?" But the Good Samaritan reversed the question, "If I do not stop to help this man, what will happen to him?" The Samaritan stopped, cared for and paid the hotel (Inn) bill for a complete stranger. He went out of his way for a man he didn't know who had been robbed, beaten, and left to die by thieves. He served a stranger, by sharing his time and financial means.

No one can do everything, but everyone can do something. Again, like the Samaritan, if we exercise this gift of helps, it blesses not only the one in

---

38 1 TIMOTHY 5:10

39 1 TIMOTHY 6:18-19 ESV

40 GALATIANS 6:9 KJV

need, but also the one who helps. In line with Biblical truth, we are blessed when we bless others:

> Give, and it will be given to you. Good measure, pressed down, shaken together, running over, will be put into your lap. For with the measure you use it will be measured back to you.
>
> —LUKE 6:38

> The saying is trustworthy, and I want you to insist on these things, so that those who have believed in God may be careful to devote themselves to good works. These things are excellent and profitable for people.
>
> —TITUS 3:8

In JOHN 6, a young boy shared his picnic with Jesus and learned a profound lesson in God's mathematics and methods. Five loaves + two fish + Jesus = five thousand people and their families fed, with twelve baskets of leftover food. Jesus turned the boy's small offering into a banquet for the masses, with leftovers in abundance.

Likewise, Mary Magdalene shared her most expensive spikenard perfume with Jesus and "wherever the gospel is proclaimed in the whole world, what she has done will be told in memory of her,"[41] even as we are doing now. When we give our all sacrificially to Jesus, He multiplies it beyond our imagination.

I cannot write about being *helps* without reflecting on Mary bearing God's Son in her womb, and Joseph of Arimathea sharing his virgin tomb, for Jesus's burial. What are you sharing in your service to our Lord and Savior, Jesus Christ?

The Bible tells us "Through love be servants of one another."[42] We should think of our service to others as an assignment from God, and this will change our perspective and our attitude. Life owes us nothing. But we choose wisely when we are quick to serve those whom God has placed before us, those who "stumble" into our path. When we are faithful in small things, we will be called to bigger things. Our Savior Christ came not to be ministered unto, but to minister, and so gave His life as a ransom for many.[43] We are destined to share His throne![44] How is your servant heart? What are you sharing for Jesus?

---

41 Mark 14:9 ESV

42 Galatians 5:13 ESV

43 Mark 10:45

44 Revelation 3:21

TAKE MY LIFE

You may be wondering how to share the truth of the Holy Spirit's gift of helps? There is a simple answer—through encouraging, loving, praying, sharing, and serving others. This truth can be shared with your home-group, contact group, youth group, prayer partners, bible study group, your wife or husband, and your children, friends and neighbors. We should not wait until we feel like doing it, but rather determine day-by-day how we are going to seek the opportunities the Lord places in our way, and empowers us through His Holy Spirit to be a blessed "helps."

> For we are his workmanship, created in Christ Jesus for good works, which God prepared beforehand, that we should walk in them.
>
> —Ephesians 2:10

You may wonder what has motivated me to write this book? Again, there is a simple answer—I've never seen another book on the gift of helps. In writing this book, I consulted widely among those I respect and admire, those believers I know to be knowledgeable and gifted in the Word and I am blessed to include their wisdom in this book, for the fullest edification of the body of Christ.

That said, there are other, more personal reasons for writing this book. Having lived a very independent, self-sufficient and successful life, there came a "Jacob" moment when God, out of His unfathomable love and unmerited favor toward me, seemed to have tired of me not putting Him first in my life. He was prominent, but not preeminent.

Our God is a jealous God and rightly seeks the fullness of our fellowship, faithfulness, and fulfilment of His Kingdom plans for us, in and through the gifts He has given us. For two years I prayed these words, "Take my life and let it be, consecrated Lord to thee."[45] He answered as only God could. He stripped me of everything. Health. Wealth. Home. He broke me in order to restore me into who I am today. My family and I lost everything, but gained so much more.

As I mentioned in the dedication, starting in April 2010 I was hospitalized on numerous occasions for depression. Humanly speaking, I may never have lived to write any book but for the fact that alongside me, one-by-one, came believers, brothers and sisters in Christ who exercised the "gift of helps", starting with my wife Susan and our sons Luke and James. My life story gives testimony to the fact that God, our loving Father,

45 Frances Havergal, Henry Malan, "Take My Life And Let It Be"

sent us very many *helps* during the difficult storms we went through. Many of those who became the greatest *helps* were people I was close to in fellowship for over thirty years, but others were complete strangers. God used friends and strangers alike, in extraordinary ways to help us. It is this personal testimony that drives the passion with which I write The Gift of Helps.

As I was talking with our son James about my experiences, he pointed out the similarity between my experience and the story of the shipwreck in Acts 27. I was broken, like Jacob, he said, the emotional and mental storm being as tumultuous as the experience that Paul and Luke had on that storm-tossed boat. And just as the *helps* aboard that boat dived overboard with ropes at great risk to secure the timber below the boat and prevent it from breaking apart (mentioned in Chapter One), so those who exercised the gift of helps around me did the same, by undergirding me with their love, prayers, and encouragement which they shared with me in so many ways.

To this day I limp from my brokenness as Jacob did, but I am profoundly grateful for the *helps* I received in so many ways. Because of this, I felt it would be selfish of me not to awaken the body of Christ to the gift of helps—the least recognized, least talked about, least exercised (knowingly) gift. To do this would make those dark and painful years of wrestling with God more than worth it.

THE RESTORATION BUSINESS

I've shared snippets from my life story above for you to see God's Word from Philippians 4:16 NLT fulfilled: "You sent help more than once." I am who I am today in Christ because of many people who gave of themselves on my behalf. I thank the Lord for each one of them continually. Each of these people exercised their gift of helps, sharing so much with my family and I.

It is my prayer that this book would lead to hundreds of thousands of believers, perhaps for the first time, coming into the fullness and realization that the Holy Spirit has given them the gift of helps and that as blessed members of the body of Christ, they begin to share this much needed ministry with others. We are to serve one another, "not by the way of eye-service, as people-pleasers, but as bondservants of Christ, doing the will of God from the heart."[46] The Holy Spirit's gift of helps is for sharing, for giving away, both to the body of Christ and beyond, as we are called to help those who cannot help themselves.

---

46 Ephesians 6:6 ESV

Allowing the Holy Spirit to lead us to the people whom we can best share our gift of *helps* with, is a key part of our purpose here on earth, whether sharing a burden, an encouraging word or a prayer. As you lend a strong arm of support to those who are sinking in life's troubles, you will see what the Lord does through you and for you, as you exercise your gift of helps.

> So then, as we have opportunity, let us do good to everyone, and especially to those who are of the household of faith.
>
> —GALATIANS 6:10

God is bigger than failure—my own testimony bears witness to that truth. He is indeed in the restoration business. He is able to do exceedingly abundantly above all that we ask or think.[47] My prayer is that God by His Spirit will use this book to prompt you into using your gift of helps, and that as the great numbers of believers share with each other the blessings of this gift, there will arise a great army of active *helps*—encouraging, loving, praying, sharing and serving, being the spiritual salt in the community, building up the body of Christ, and making a difference in the lives of

---

47 EPHESIANS 3:20

many. As this book has joyfully expressed, as you become a blessing, so you will be blessed.

Final Thoughts

CONCLUSION

The Gift of Helps is a gift of the Holy Spirit. Having come to recognize it in my own life, I am passionate about sharing, because it can make such a difference in the lives of all who come to know it, whether giving or receiving. In the pages of this small book, I hope I have sufficiently introduced you to the gift of helps so you may become a daily blessing to others, as you exercise this gift. I would encourage you to pray and ask the Holy Spirit to release the fullness of the gift of helps in you, because you so very much want to be in the ministry of *helps*.

In writing this book I have shared the desire I have for a life that fulfils God's plan and purpose for me. I want nothing but God's fullest blessing and I'm sure that's the case for you too. As you come to understand the gift of helps, it's not too late to activate it and confer God's blessing upon others. Joel 2:25 NIV says, "I will repay you for the years the locusts have eaten." Be assured, "for God's gifts and his call are irrevocable."[48]

As you've read my personal stories in this book, I hope you've understood that they have been included to show how real God is, how ready to empower and bless us beyond anything we could have ever imagined. He is the ultimate manifestation of the gift of helps and He calls on His children, you and me, to share that gift of His Spirit as a witness and testimony to His Lordship in our lives. I can testify that as you exercise the gift of helps, God will resource and reward you; as we read in Ezekiel 34:26 KJV, "There shall be showers of blessing."

> My one purpose in life is to help people find a personal relationship with God, which I believe comes from knowing Christ.
>
> —Billy Graham

Who are you helping by sharing the Gospel with them? You never know how many people may come up to you in heaven and say, "thank you for exercising your gift of helps."

---

48 Romans 11:29 NIV

Our daily prayer can be: *So help me Lord Jesus, and empower me blessed Holy Spirit, to manifest your gift of helps daily as you lead. Amen.*

Lightning Source UK Ltd.
Milton Keynes UK
UKHW010641090622
404134UK00006B/762

9 781913 771003